T0278368

EVOLUTION & CULTURAL INFLUENCES OF MUSIC

COUNTRY

EVOLUTION & CULTURAL INFLUENCES OF MUSIC

COUNTRY

ELECTRONIC DANCE MUSIC (EDM)

HIP-HOP

LATIN AND CARIBBEAN

POP MUSIC

R&B, SOUL, AND GOSPEL

ROCK

STAGE AND SCREEN

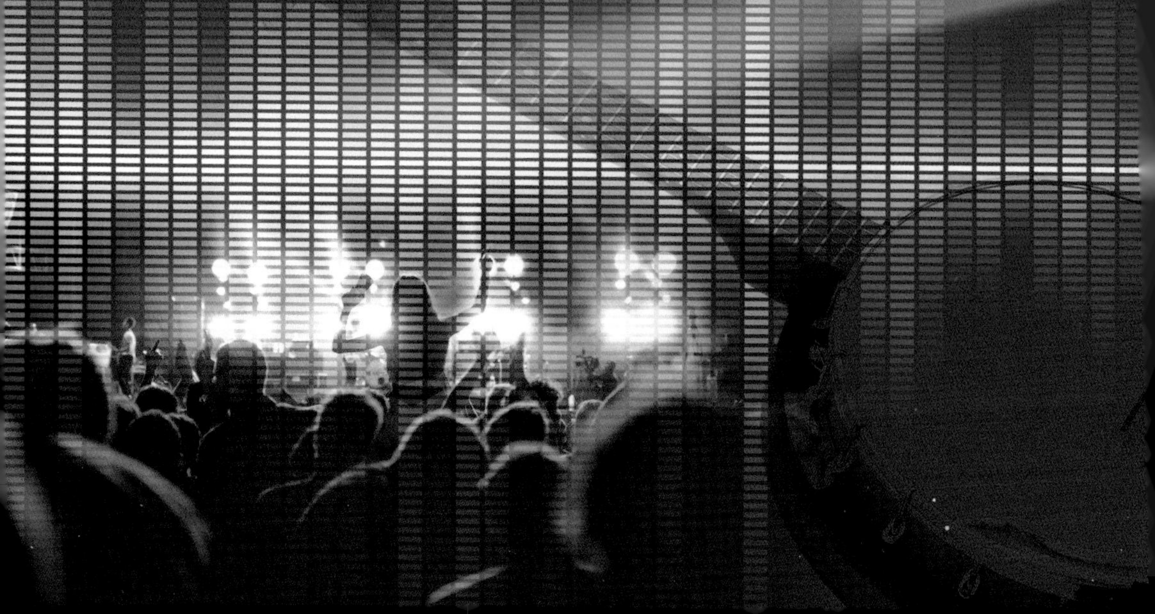

EVOLUTION & CULTURAL INFLUENCES OF MUSIC

COUNTRY

JOYCE A. ANTHONY

MASON CREST

PHILADELPHIA | MIAMI

MASON CREST

450 Parkway Drive, Suite D, Broomall, Pennsylvania 19008
(866) MCP-BOOK (toll-free) • www.masoncrest.com

© 2020 by Mason Crest, an imprint of National Highlights, Inc.

All rights reserved. No part of this publication may be reproduced or transmitted in any form or by any means, electronic or mechanical, including photocopying, recording, taping, or any information storage and retrieval system, without permission from the publisher.

Printed and bound in the United States of America.

CPSIA Compliance Information: Batch #ECIM2019.
For further information, contact Mason Crest at 1-866-MCP-Book.

First printing

ISBN (hardback) 978-1-4222-4370-1
ISBN (series) 978-1-4222-4369-5
ISBN (ebook) 978-1-4222-7435-4

Library of Congress Cataloging-in-Publication Data on file at the Library of Congress.

Interior and cover design: Torque Advertising + Design
Production: Michelle Luke

Publisher's Note: Websites listed in this book were active at the time of publication. The publisher is not responsible for websites that have changed their address or discontinued operation since the date of publication. The publisher reviews and updates the websites each time the book is reprinted.

QR CODES AND LINKS TO THIRD-PARTY CONTENT

You may gain access to certain third-party content ("Third-Party Sites") by scanning and using the QR Codes that appear in this publication (the "QR Codes"). We do not operate or control in any respect any information, products, or services on such Third-Party Sites linked to by us via the QR Codes included in this publication, and we assume no responsibility for any materials you may access using the QR Codes. Your use of the QR Codes may be subject to terms, limitations, or restrictions set forth in the applicable terms of use or otherwise established by the owners of the Third-Party Sites. Our linking to such Third-Party Sites via the QR Codes does not imply an endorsement or sponsorship of such Third-Party Sites or the information, products, or services offered on or through the Third-Party Sites, nor does it imply an endorsement or sponsorship of this publication by the owners of such Third-Party Sites.

CONTENTS

KEY ICONS TO LOOK FOR:

Words to Understand: These words with their easy-to-understand definitions will increase the reader's understanding of the text while building vocabulary skills.

Sidebars: This boxed material within the main text allows readers to build knowledge, gain insights, explore possibilities, and broaden their perspectives by weaving together additional information to provide realistic and holistic perspectives.

Educational videos: Readers can view videos by scanning our QR codes, providing them with additional educational content to supplement the text. Examples include news coverage, moments in history, speeches, iconic sports moments, and much more!

Text-Dependent Questions: These questions send the reader back to the text for more careful attention to the evidence presented there.

Research Projects: Readers are pointed toward areas of further inquiry connected to each chapter. Suggestions are provided for projects that encourage deeper research and analysis.

Series Glossary of Key Terms: This back-of-the-book glossary contains terminology used throughout this series. Words found here increase the reader's ability to read and comprehend higher-level books and articles in this field.

Luke Bryan is one of the most popular country music performers today. Fourteen of his songs have hit number one on the country music charts.

 ## WORDS TO UNDERSTAND

acoustic—a musical instrument that does not have electrical amplification.

Appalachia—a name for a region of the United States that is located around the Appalachian Mountain range, particularly in parts of the states of New York, Pennsylvania, Ohio, Kentucky, North and South Carolina, Tennessee, Virginia, West Virginia, Georgia, and Alabama.

chord—a group of three or more music notes that create harmony.

CHAPTER 1

Origins of Country Music

What do you picture when you hear the words "country music?" If you don't normally listen to this music, you might imagine men in overalls stomping one foot and singing in a twangy voice while someone plays a banjo or fiddle. If you have had some exposure to the music, you may picture someone in jeans and a cowboy hat holding an **acoustic** guitar and singing something about his woman leaving him, or about drinking, or both. If you are a fan of country music and have a good idea of what it is, however, you realized that it is these things but it is also a whole lot more. Regardless of where you stand in your knowledge of country music, you will find that the music you listen to today is more than likely to have found its roots in this form of music. Let's start our journey by taking a look at what exactly makes a song country music.

The Lyrics

Ask any country music fan and they will tell you that the most important element in any country song is the lyrics. In country music, every song tells a story. Sometimes the story is just a small glimpse into a part of some environment, such as a small town, or a moment in life, such as the feeling at the exact moment someone walks away.

Many country songs speak about things that the singer has learned. For example, the Garth Brooks song "The Dance" is sung from the perspective of a man whose romantic relationship has ended. The singer says he could have avoided the heartache of breaking up if he had only known in advance what would happen. However, he goes onto to say, that he was better off not knowing because otherwise he would also have missed some of the most special moments in his life.

The lyrics of country songs are easy for many people to relate to. They describe emotions that everyone feels, even if the events aren't familiar. They also often express the major events that are happening in the world around us. After the September 11, 2001, terrorist attacks on the United States, there were many country songs that said Americans wouldn't be broken or defeated. Many songs include a patriotic message, one that supports the country and government. This trend of patriotism helped to divide country music from the earlier folk music genre in the 1960s and 1970s.

The lyrics of country music also speak of the working man. In the beginning, many songs involved railroad workers, cowboys, or coal miners. Over the years, songs have been written about Americans with other occupations, such as truck drivers and factory workers. Country songs often extoll the **virtues** of working hard, raising a family, and helping others.

Women who sing country music often express their own attitudes. Some sing romantic love songs, like singers in other musical genres, but others have more sass. One of Loretta Lynn's early hits, "Fist City," was sung from the perspective of a angry woman who was threatening to beat up another woman for "lovin' my man." More recently, singers like Jo Dee Messina and Carrie Underwood scored big hits with songs about cheating boyfriends. Many country songs today depict strong women who

Many country songs reflect patriotic values, such as Chely Wright's 2005 hit "The Bumper of My SUV," which expresses support for American soldiers serving overseas.

know they have power over their lives and aren't willing to sit back and let their partner have all the fun.

Fun is an important aspect of country music. Artists like Sheb Wooley and Ray Stevens created comedic songs that gave listeners a chance to laugh and forget about their daily hardships. Country music isn't all about the suffering and hardship in life that many think it is. It is about life as a whole, and this always includes moments of fun and laughter.

"Songwriting is fragile and yet through it all, it's the most important step in music," Garth Brooks once commented on the importance of lyrics to country music. "If we don't have songwriters, there's not going to be a music business."

Simple Melodies

One of the first things listeners notice about a country music tune is how simple the melodies are. Most songs are based on three basic **chords**, G-C-D or G-D-A. There are variations in the order of the chords and there are others in some of the music but these are the two that are most prevalent. The tempo changes from slow and bluesy to upbeat dance music, but the chords remain the same.

This similarity developed mainly due to the instruments available when country music first began being played. The simple string instruments that were available in **Appalachia** during the early twentieth century—particularly the American fiddle and banjo—didn't allow for complicated combinations. This didn't matter much, however, as the performers focus more on the lyrics. Modern songwriters continue to draw on these simple medleys. They have worked for years, so why change a good thing?

Originally, country music was performed by musicians with American fiddles, banjos, guitars, and harmonicas. These instruments were readily available and traveled easily. In fact, poor Americans in rural areas could make simple instruments themselves. The banjo and harmonica were originally introduced by African-American settlers or slaves in the Appalachia area, while white settlers from Europe brought or created instruments familiar to their home countries.

It wasn't until the 1930s that drums began to accompany country and western songs. Brass horns and woodwind instruments were for "city folk," and didn't find their way into the country music scene for quite a few years. Even today, it is rare that you find horns other than an occasional saxophone being used. Pianos started appearing in the 1940s and 1950s.

Where Country Music Started

The Appalachian Mountains have always been home to a wide variety of immigrants. The original white immigrants to the area came from England, Wales, Scotland, and Ireland. They didn't bring much with them, but they brought their music.

Black slaves in the Caribbean created the banjo in the seventeenth century, and their descendants brought the instrument to America. They could easily be made from gourds or other materials, and used to play simple melodies.

Traditional English ballads and Irish/Scottish folk songs were prevalent. Another group that found their way to this area were slaves and freed blacks. They also didn't have much in the way of material belongings but they had their own African-influenced musical styles. The musical styles meshed well, and marked the origins of modern country music.

African Americans brought harmonicas and banjos to Appalachia, while the Irish and Scots had their version of the violin, which became known as the American fiddle. Guitars could be constructed from materials that were easily found. Every so often, bagpipes made an appearance but that was never a large part of the country music tradition.

Most of those who lived in Appalachia were poor. During the nineteenth century, many men earned a hard living by working on railroads or deep in coal mines. Life was hard and the easiest

Scan here to learn more about the origins of country music:

Life in Appalachia during the early twentieth century was hard, and many people turned to music to relax after working long, hard hours in coal mines.

way to wind down after a long, difficult day was to gather on someone's porch to play music, sing, and dance. Even today, many of the dances that accompany country songs can be traced back to traditional Irish jigs.

These musicians had a strong faith that kept them going, and you could hear this in the heartfelt Christian hymns they sang. Even today, many country music artists include at least one spiritual when they perform a concert. The songs that arose spoke of everyday life for that was what mattered to those who performed. Love, family, work, and faith all were popular subjects. Most of those who lived in this area could go months without hearing of events that were taking place in the rest of the world. When they did hear of something major, that too was incorporated in the music.

When some of these early music-makers decided to try to make a better life for their families, they headed south or west, taking their music with them. This made it possible for others to hear the unique blending of traditional folk music and African blues. The term "hillbilly music" was often applied because the genre had originated in the mountains. From this beginning of a simple way to bring enjoyment and relaxation into a hard life, one of the longest lasting genres of music was born.

Growing and Changing

Beginning in the early 1920s, record players and radio broadcasts enabled Americans all over the country to hear different regional styles of music. The "hillbilly music" of Appalachia soon moved to the recording studios of Georgia and Tennessee.

One of the first big stars was Vernon Dalhart, whose 1924 recording of "The Wreck of the Old '97" sold more than a million copies. He recorded thousands of other popular songs. Jimmie Rodgers was another popular performer. The first women to record country songs were Aunt Samantha Bumgarner, a fiddler and singer, who was accompanied by Eva Davis on guitar. In 1925, Nashville radio station WSM began broadcasting a one-hour show of country music that became known as the Grand Ole Opry.

The Great Depression of the 1930s hurt record sales, but radio became even more popular as people tuned in to find an escape from their everyday hardships. This helped spread country music even further. The Grand Ole Opry show continued to thrive, expanding to four hours and attracting

The Grand Ole Opry theater in Nashville has been an iconic symbol of country music since the 1920s.

the most popular country music artists. In Texas, musician and bandleader Bob Wills blended popular jazz rhythms with country melodies to create "western swing." He was among the first to add drums to his band, the Texas Playboys. This popular style won favor not only in the West but also in front of audiences in New York City and the Midwest, where dance clubs were

DEFORD BAILEY

DeFord Bailey (1899–1982) was one of the most
popular African-American country music
artists of the 1920s and 1930s.
He was a regular performer
on a weekly radio show
broadcast from Nashville,
Tennessee, that is known
today as the Grand Ole Opry.
In fact, some historians say
that his performances actually
inspired the show's famous name.
Bailey played other instruments,
but he was particularly known for
his distinctive style of harmonica
playing. He performed with white
country music stars, but faced
racial discrimination off the
stage, especially in the
southern states.

springing up everywhere.

By the 1940s, western movies were drawing crowds and contributing new influences to country music. Roy Rogers and Gene Autry were among the most popular performers of "cowboy songs" that spoke of life in the wide open spaces of the western states, riding the range and living free as the wind. Another popular singer and songwriter during this period was Hank Williams. His "honky-tonk" style would exert a strong influence on many other musicians, such as Elvis Presley and Johnny Cash.

During the 1960s, the country music genre continued to change. Folk musicians were less likely to support the government or the American military involvement in Vietnam. They sang protest songs, as well as songs about love and gentler times. Country performers like Merle Haggard ridiculed the protesters and the hippie culture of the late 1960s, and extolled patriotism and the values of small-town America.

During the 1970s, country music producers in Nashville began to incorporate pop music elements into the songs. This enabled country artists like John Denver, Tammy Wynette, and Glen Campbell to release cross-over hits that appealed to easy listening audiences on pop radio stations. At the same time, another form that came to be known as "outlaw country" attracted listeners who felt they were marginalized by society. Singers like Willie Nelson, Waylon Jennings, and Hank Williams Jr. sang gritty songs with rock influences about low-class people who worked hard and played harder.

Country music has continued to evolve. Some performers tried to return to the original sounds of the genre. Others have incorporated hip-hop into mainstream country songs. The lines between adult contemporary music, classic rock, and country music have become blurred as many artists enjoy broader audiences. As the country becomes more diverse, the country music industry has begun to embrace the differences to show

Award-winning singer/songwriter Garth Brooks has sold more albums than any performer in American history. His music dominated the country charts in the 1990s and early 2000s.

Members of the LGBTQ+ community have performed country music for many years, even though few chose to come out publicly until recently. One of the first openly gay country music groups was Lavender Country. Their first song was seen as almost a parody but in 1972, they came out with their first openly gay album. This group's musical style takes one back to the early days of bluegrass but the lyrics remind us of the struggles facing those in the LGBTQ+ community in the seventies. Other well-known LGBTQ country performers include k.d. lang, Chely Wright, and Ty Herndon.

that people from different backgrounds can get along.

From its origins in Appalachia, country music has spread throughout the world. Its simple messages full of emotion appeal to humans everywhere. Country music may have evolved from simple mountain tunes, but in the family tree of music it remains the sturdy roots from which many other American genres have emerged.

TEXT-DEPENDENT QUESTIONS

1. Where did the banjo originate?
2. What was the first country music hit and who recorded it?
3. What does every country song do with its lyrics?

RESEARCH PROJECT

Many of the first instruments in country music were made from materials that were lying around. Have fun making your own banjo by following the instructions here https://ourpastimes.com/banjos-can-make-pie-tins-6025685.html. What other materials do you think may have been used in the mountains in the early 1900s? Can you try your hand at a homemade guitar? What differences are there between the banjo and the guitar?

Members of the Bog Trotters band perform the traditional hill-billy music of the Appalachian region, 1937. Pictured are band leader Doc Davis with autoharp, Alex Dunford and Crockett Ward with fiddles, Wade Ward with banjo, and Fields Ward with guitar.

 WORDS TO UNDERSTAND

duet—a song or other piece of music sung or played by two people.

hub—center of activity

variation—a different or distinct form or version of something.

venue—arena for staging an event

CHAPTER 2

Growing Stronger

From the Appalachian Mountains to the world, country music has come a long way from its humble beginnings. Many people consider Nashville, Tennessee, to be the birthplace of modern country music, but it was not the actual **hub** for country music in the earliest years. Recordings were made first in New York City, but it soon became clear that with all the talented musicians coming out of the mountains and the western states, music producers needed to find a place that was easier for them to get to. That place became Atlanta in the 1920s and early 1930s.

In this chapter we will be exploring the first years of what would later become one of the most popular genres of music in the world. We will visit with some of the early superstars and take a look into what shaped the world of country music. You'll meet some people you have heard about and some that most of the world has forgotten. Each was essential in helping spread the word that country music was here to stay.

A Boy With a Dream

We all have dreams while we are growing up. In many cases, those dreams remain hidden in the backs of our minds, waiting for someday. It takes courage and a willingness to fail to act on those dreams. It becomes even more difficult when nobody else seems to share those dreams. What many people never realize is there are many out there who may share the same

Fiddle player Eck Robertson was one of the first people to record country music songs, in 1922.

dream but they are waiting for someone else to make that first move. Eck Robertson was someone who was willing to make a move to realize his dream even though he didn't see anyone else doing the same.

Eck Robertson loved playing the fiddle and wanted to share his joy with everyone who would listen. He gathered his few belongings and set out in 1920 to see if he could get others to enjoy the fiddle as much as he did. Traveling by foot most of the time, he played in small towns that were willing to give him a spot to stand and time to play. His audiences started to grow as he made his way across the Midwest toward the one place where dreams came true, New York City.

Along the way, Eck teamed up with another fiddler and they convinced an executive at the Victor Talking Machine Company in New York City to give them a recording session. On June 30, 1922, they entered the studio and recorded two songs together. The producer enjoyed Eck's playing so much he invited the young fiddler to return alone the next day and record on his own. During this second section, Eck Robertson recorded the classic "Sally Gooden." He recorded the original song, as well as twelve **variations**. This is still one of the most played fiddle tunes in the world today. Even John Denver mentioned playing "Sally Gooden" in his hit "Thank God I'm a Country Boy."

Atlanta Gains Attention

As Eck Robertson was making his way to New York City, another fiddler named John Carson was also touring. His playing centered around the Atlanta, Georgia, area. After several years of playing every small **venue** he could find, John Carson started to hear about Eck Robertson and wanted to take his own music dreams to the next level. In 1923, in an abandoned building in Atlanta, he set up what equipment he could find and recorded two sides of a record.

Fiddlin' John Carson is at the right in this photo of 1920s musicians meeting in Tennessee. Others pictured include Al Hopkins, Joe Hopkins, Elvis Alderman, John Rector, and "Uncle" Am Stewart.

The record was good enough that music producers in New York City recognized his talent. They invited "Fiddlin' John Carson" to make more records. Between 1923 and 1935, he made more than 150 records. Two of them were major hits, selling more than a million copies. Carson's success made the world take notice of the Atlanta music scene, and this Southern city soon became the destination for those looking to make their mark in country music. Atlanta would remain the center of country music activity until the 1930s.

Scan here to see how records were made in 1922:

Country Music's First Family

In the 1930s, a married couple by the names of A.P. and Sarah Carter joined forces with their sister-in-law, Maybelle Carter. This trio set out to see if they could interest a recording company in making records of their act. Between the three of them, they sang and played a host of instruments and the sound was as pure as any coming out of the Appalachians. They caught the interest of a new recording studio in Nashville, and the Carter Family became one of the most popular acts to help spread country music. They toured and recorded until 1943, putting out a total of 300 recordings.

When the original trio split in 1943, "Mother" Maybelle, as she had come to be called, continued touring. Her new group consisted of her and her three young daughters, Helen, Anita, and June. The pure harmony they produced made them the

MAYBELLE   A.P.   SARA

A.P. Carter (center), his wife Sara (right), and their sister-in-law Maybelle (left) had several hits performing as the Carter Family during the 1920s and 1930s. Some of their songs would become country music standards, like "Wabash Cannonball" and "Can the Circle Be Unbroken?"

favorites of all who heard their music. Eventually, the touring slowed down as life took these women in other directions but they never totally quit country music. The youngest daughter, June, would eventually marry Johnny Cash, another up-and-coming country singer and they recorded **duets** together. Today, their children and grandchildren continue to have a strong presence in country music.

Hank Williams had eleven hits during his career, which ended short because of his drinking and hard-living ways. His contribution to the country music industry is still in play today because of his songwriting. Hank is credited with either writing or co-writing 167 songs, all before his death at the age of twenty-nine. Singers both new and old are still singing these masterpieces. Today, his son, Hank Williams Jr., is carrying on the country music tradition. His grandson, Hank Williams III, is also a singer whose style alternates between outlaw country, punk rock, and metal.

Radio Spreads the Music

During the 1930s and 1940s, two major things happened that would change the country music world. During the 1930s, the United States suffered through the Great Depression. In 1941, the US became involved in World War II. Both of these events had an effect on entertainment in America.

The Great Depression was a time of economic hardship. Factories and businesses closed, and many people lost their jobs. In the worst years, more than 25 percent of Americans were unemployed. Droughts in the midwestern states of the Great Plains ruined farms, forcing people to leave their homes move elsewhere.

The hard times meant that most people could no longer afford such luxuries as buying records or attending nightclubs and concert halls to hear performers. Instead, for entertainment people turned to radio broadcasts. Families could sit around their radio in the evening and listen to their favorite singers without having to spend money. For fans of country music, one of the most popular radio shows was called the Grand Ole Opry. The weekly programs were broadcast across the country, taking country music into areas where it had never been before.

In 1942, singer Roy Acuff and songwriter Fred Rose joined together to create Acuff-Rose Publications. They chose Nashville as the base of operation. Country musicians and songwriters started making their way to this city and it seemed like the perfect location to set up a place for barn dances, as the performances were called so the Ryman Auditorium was built to host the Grand Ole Opry. Country singers both old and young vied for a chance to perform there, knowing that their career would get a much-needed boost.

As American soldiers fought a war overseas, those still at home looked for ways to boost their morale. The Grand Ole Opry took to the seas, sending musicians to perform for the soldiers in Europe and the Pacific. This was the first time most people outside this country had been exposed to this type of music and it soon became a favorite. The familiar topics and friendly faces brought a much-needed piece of home to the battle-weary soldiers and our Allies.

Cowboy Country and Western Swing

During the thirties and forties, another form of entertainment was becoming popular and it was to create yet another branch of country music. This was the increasing popularity of the movie

Jimmy Rodgers is pictured wearing the uniform of a railroad worker in this 1928 publicity photo. The "singing brakeman" was the best-selling artist of the Victor recording company from the mid-1920s until his death at age thirty-five due to complications from tuberculosis.

The economic problems of the Great Depression were made worse for farmers living in the southern Great Plains by severe droughts during the mid-1930s. Dust storms like this one swept the region from Texas to Nebraska. People and livestock were killed and crops failed, forcing many farm families to migrate West in search of work and better living conditions.

theater, and Western films in particular. Children and adults could pay a few cents and spend all day watching cowboys round up cattle, camp by the light of the Moon, and go about their day on a ranch. Many people dreamed of a life with few or no fences. A life where every day wasn't spent going to work in a mine or a factory for little pay that barely kept their families fed and clothed seemed ideal.

The on-screen cowboys often sang songs about life on the open range. The tunes were often accompanied by very little instrumentation—often, a simple acoustic guitar was all that could be heard. The lyrics were simple stories of freedom that appealed to many people. The tunes were slow, adding to the peaceful feeling. Movie stars such as Gene Autry and Roy Rogers

Bob Wills and his Texas Playboys pose with Gene Autry (wearing hat; Wills is to the right of Autry), circa 1938.

roped cattle, fought outlaws, and added fuel to many dreams in the audience.

Meanwhile, Texas singer and bandleader Bob Wills was creating still another modified version of country music. His music was a combination of jazz music, which was popular in the big cities, and the country music he had grown up with. He fused the two together, creating what came to be known as Western Swing. Bob Wills was among the first to incorporate the piano into country music. The up-tempo beats made dancing popular and most weekends would find people around the state, and eventually around the country, grabbing a partner and dancing the Texas Two-Step. Country music was gaining an even wider audience.

Music Explosion

As the forties were winding down, country music was becoming known all over the United States. Various branches had sprung from the traditional mountain sound. Bluegrass and Country became more divided, sometimes coming together but getting more diversified. No longer called by the term "hillbilly music," country and western music had firmly found its way into the music arena.

If people were amazed at how far it had come in thirty years, they would be even more amazed at what the next forty had in store as Memphis and California made their mark and a brand new genre that would rival country music entered the scene.

TEXT-DEPENDENT QUESTIONS

1. Who is credited with making the first official country music recording?
2. How many songs did Hank Williams write before his death?
3. What types of music were blended to create the Western Swing sound?

RESEARCH PROJECT

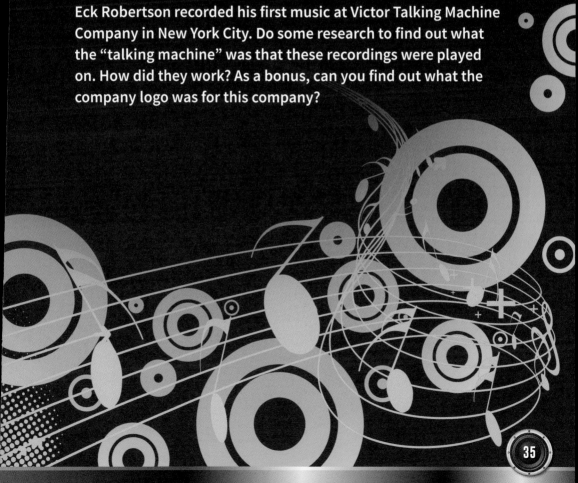

Eck Robertson recorded his first music at Victor Talking Machine Company in New York City. Do some research to find out what the "talking machine" was that these recordings were played on. How did they work? As a bonus, can you find out what the company logo was for this company?

In the early 1980s, George Strait helped to return country music to its traditional roots. Since 1982, forty-five of Strait's songs have reached #1 on the country music charts—more chart-toppers than any other artist in any musical genre.

 ## WORDS TO UNDERSTAND

baby boomers—a term for the generation born between 1946 and 1964. Many of these children came of age in the 1950s and 1960s, and helped shape popular culture.

fruition—bring to life

manifest—become reality

CHAPTER 3

Going Mainstream

The 1950s and 1960s was a time of great change in the United States. Americans had emerged from the Great Depression and won World War II in 1945. Millions of soldiers returned home after the war, married, and began starting families and building a strong country for their children. The world held promise for the youth of the fifties.

As the children born after the war—known as the **baby boomers**—became teenagers, they wanted to put aside the old ways of their parents. This generation knew there was more to life than just working hard, and they wanted to experience everything. One of the ways this new, fun-loving mindset showed the most was in music. The baby boomers didn't want to hear music that spoke of hardship and country living. They wanted music that allowed them to dance with abandon. White teens quickly discovered the blues and jazz music that was often performed by black Americans. Ray Charles was making a name for himself in the emerging genre known as R&B (rhythm and blues). The baby boomers soon became the major music buyers of their time.

With bluegrass and traditional country artists losing their audience, those in charge of the music industry started to look for ways to meet the demands of these baby boomers. As they were trying to determine where to go next, country performers were also trying to adapt to the changing times.

The Bakersfield Sound

California isn't a place most people would connect with country music, even today. However, during the 1930s farmers from states like Oklahoma and Arkansas left the Great Plains and moved to California due to droughts and dust storms. They brought their music with them.

Bakersfield, California, was a town full of workers. After work, and on the weekends, they wanted to relax. Like the young people of the time, these men and women wanted to let loose after a hard work day. They wanted to dance and enjoy life as

Dust Bowl refugees found jobs as farm workers in California. They brought their music with them. A California variation known as the "Bakersfield Sound" would have a huge impact on the country music genre.

To learn more about the Bakersfield sound, scan here:

much as they could. The slow, idealistic songs of traditional country didn't allow this. The noise in the bars and nightclubs of Bakersfield also made it difficult for traditional country performers to be heard.

The Bakersfield performers began replacing their acoustic instruments with the electric guitars that were beginning to appear on the music scene. These guitars could be played loud, allowing the music to be heard above a noisy crowd. They also better suited the newer lyrics that spoke to the average working man.

This new sound, the Bakersfield Sound, was easy to dance to and spoke of the experience of the working man, from the hard life on an assembly line to the pleasure of a night out drinking and dancing. It wasn't a smooth, polished sound like the country music coming out of Nashville. Instead, the singers often had raspy voices that had been altered with alcohol and

Country music legend Buck Owens (right) attended the 2003 ceremony when Dwight Yoakam received a star on the Hollywood Walk of Fame.

cigarettes. Two early performers of the Bakersfield Sound were Merle Haggard, who later become part of the Outlaw Country sub-genre, and Buck Owens. Today, country fans can still hear the Bakersfield influence in performers like Dwight Yoakam.

Meanwhile in Memphis

The year was 1954 and an unknown music producer opened up a small recording studio in Memphis, Tennessee. Sam Phillips felt that Nashville was too full of country artists at the time, and felt Memphis would be a great place to work on bringing a vision he had to **fruition**. It was with this vision that he started Sun Records, and set to work.

Sam Phillips felt that music was a way to highlight the similarities between the races and bring them together. He knew that the odds of finding a black recording artist that could help bridge this gap was next to impossible in an age where black artists still weren't getting the recognition they deserved. What he wanted to find was a white country boy who could sing in a rhythm and blues style. It was his belief that by combining country roots with a black sound, he would create something that was relatable to a wider audience than either alone could reach. When a shy, nineteen-year-old country boy entered his office, Phillips came to believe his vision would **manifest**.

Elvis Presley in 1954 was far from a superstar. His humble manner and so-so guitar-playing skills didn't speak of star material. His soulful voice, however, captured the attention of Sam Phillips. For a while, Sam was about to give up and keep looking for his special talent. Elvis didn't seem to be more than mediocre on anything he tried to sing. He was nervous and seemed to be struggling. Sam could tell he was putting his entire effort into doing well but the magic wasn't happening. After a long session of poor results, everyone took a break. Young Elvis remembered a blues song he had heard at one point and started

Although Elvis Presley is remembered as the "king of rock and roll," many of his earliest releases were hits on both the country and pop music charts. He returned to his country roots in the mid-1970s, releasing several albums that were popular among country fans. In February 1977 his song "Moody Blue" reached #1 on the Billboard country singles chart, making it Elvis's final #1 hit during his lifetime.

Most people think of Ray Charles as a master of soul music. During his career, which lasted from 1947 to 2004, he was considered the originator of soul and his music style covered blues, soul, and R&B. What many people don't know is that Ray Charles recorded four country albums between 1962 and 1970, and had eight Top-40 hits on the country music charts. Even in his later years, he still loved to pair up with country music greats occasionally. One example of this was his recording of "Seven Spanish Angels" with Willie Nelson, which was a #1 country hit in 1984.

having fun with it. The song was "That's All Right Mama." The band saw a magic spark and picked up their instruments. Before the song was over, Sam Phillips knew he'd found the magic he was seeking. All it had taken was the right song, and for Elvis to stop trying too hard and simply be himself.

This session was the start of a brand new type of country music, a fusion of blues and country that came to be known as Rockabilly. This sub-genre came to be embraced by artists such as Chuck Berry, Carl Perkins, Jerry Lee Lewis, and Roy Orbison. It was Rockabilly that would eventually morph into Rock-n-Roll.

Many people agree that if Hank Williams was the biggest male influence on country music, then Patsy Cline was the most influential female. Both of these stars died young, at the height of their fame.

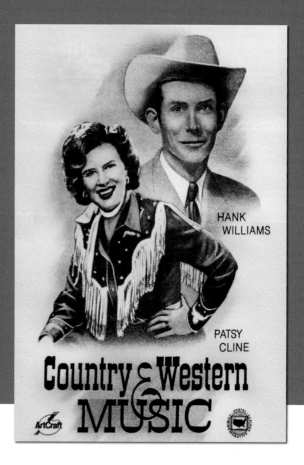

HANK WILLIAMS

PATSY CLINE

Country & Western MUSIC

ArtCraft

Female Country Music Pioneers

During the 1950s and 1960s, a few pioneering women made their mark in country music, paving the way for the many female stars to come later. Kitty Wells was the first female solo artist to achieve fame in country music. She started singing in her teenage years, but didn't gain attention until she was in her her early thirties, when she recorded "It Wasn't God Who Made Honky Tonk Angels." Wells's gingham dresses signaled the sort of quiet cooperation expected of women in the fifties, but the lyrics of her song shocked the country industry. Despite being banned by the Grand Ole Opry, the song sold a million copies and was a #1 hit. Her success showed that country music fans were ready for songs from a woman's point of view.

One of the biggest stars of the late 1950s and early 1960s was Patsy Cline. Her biggest hits included "Walkin' After Midnight," "I Fall to Pieces," and "Crazy." She was one of the few country singers of the time whose songs also appeared on the pop music charts. Her powerful voice captivated audiences wherever she went. Tragically, her career was cut short when she died in a plane crash in 1963. Ten years later, she became the first woman inducted into the Country Music Hall of Fame.

"Hank [Williams] had just passed away, and when Patsy got a record deal, rock and roll came along and stole the spotlight away from country," recalls performer Jason Petty. "That left Patsy with the challenge of having to come up with a new sound, since the twangy, honky tonk style wasn't selling records anymore. So, Patsy developed a style to satisfy both country and pop fans, something we would call 'crossover' music today. Patsy was the first to have a presence on the pop charts with a sound that featured more strings and more background vocals. The Jordanaires, who sang backup for Elvis, sang on her records giving them a deep, velvety sound. So, Patsy got country back on its feet and saved the industry at a time when it looked like all or nothing for it."

After becoming successful, Cline befriended and encouraged other young women who wanted to sing country music. One of them was Loretta Lynn. She had been born in rural Kentucky, in the very mountains that had been the birthplace of country music. Lynn had grown up poor, gotten married at age fifteen, and had four children before she turned twenty-one. However, her husband believed in her musical talent, and encouraged her to go to Nashville. She wrote songs about being a mother ("One's on the Way"), and about the problems she faced in her marriage ("Don't Come Home a Drinkin' with Lovin' on your Mind"). In her songs, she conveyed the message that she was a strong woman who would not allow a man to take advantage of her. "Coal Miner's Daughter," showing pride in her family and her upbringing, is one of Lynn's most famous songs.

Loretta Lynn received the Presidential Medal of Freedom, the nation's highest civilian honor, from President Barack Obama in 2013.

Dolly Parton started her career in Nashville as a songwriter, penning hits for Kitty Wells and others. In 1967, she began performing with Porter Wagoner, a popular singer who hosted a television show. They recorded many duets that became country hits. In the early 1970s she emerged as a solo star, with hits like "I Will Always Love You." By the end of the decade, she was a crossover star, with hits on the country and pop charts.

One of the best-selling songs by a female country singer was 1968's "Stand by Your Man," by Tammy Wynette. She had many other big hits in the late 1960s and 1970s. Many of these songs dealt with the problems that women faced: loneliness, divorce, and the hardships of everyday life. Wynette was married for several years to George Jones, a male country star, and they recorded several hit duets.

The Birth of Country Rock

The seventies brought about still more changes in country music. The first has been credited to a singer and musician born in Florida and raised in Georgia named Gram Parsons. Gram didn't consider himself a country singer, because he felt his music belonged in a category unlike any other. He referred to his blend of country, rhythm and blues, folk, soul, and rock as "Cosmic American Music." He never had much success where selling albums was concerned because his music was considered "too country" for rock stations and "too rock" for country stations. His influence, however, has been repeatedly acknowledged by musicians of both genres. So, how did Parsons hit upon this unique style that came to be called Country Rock by the rest of the world?

Gram Parsons was first influenced by Elvis Presley and was determined he liked the rock music until he went to college. Here he was introduced to the smoky Bakersfield sound of Merle Haggard and started to listen to the folk music of the Kingston Trio. He practiced combining the three sounds and when he left college, he headed out toward California. Once in California, Parsons played with a rock band called the Byrds. Their album *Sweetheart of the Rodeo* (1968) is often considered the first example of Country Rock.

When the Byrds broke up, Parsons formed a new band, the Flying Burrito Brothers, which gave him an opportunity to showcase his unique style. In time, the Flying Burrito Brothers also split up, and Parsons took some time off. That is, until he met up-and-coming folk/country singer Emmylou Harris in 1970. The two of them found that their voices blended so well that they recorded together and went on tour. As they were starting

Dolly Parton was one of country's biggest stars during the 1970s and 1980s. During her long career, twenty-five of her songs reached #1 on the country music charts, including "I Will Always Love You," "Here You Come Again," and "Islands in the Stream," a duet with Kenny Rodgers.

to be recognized, Parsons died in 1973. He was just twenty-six years old. Today, many people call Gram Parsons the "Father of Country Rock," because of the influence his musical style had on such popular bands as the Eagles, the Grateful Dead, the Marshall Tucker Band, and the Allman Brothers Band.

The Age of the Crossover

As the seventies came into full swing, country artists were starting to find it more difficult to hold their audience. This was especially true of the younger generation. This segment of the

population was divided between the rockers, the R&B fans, and folk music, which had by now separated from its country roots. There were plenty of older country entertainers who held onto the pure country style and they had fans who had followed them for years, but capturing new fans from the younger crowd was what producers and the younger singers wanted.

A new style of country song began to appear. This sound had smoother lyrics, less talk about farms, and musical accompaniment that contained less fiddle and more guitar. It appealed to many people who were in their twenties and thirties, who didn't like the sounds of hard rock groups. They had also gotten past the rebellious stage of "finding themselves" that many went through previously, so folk music became a background thing. Most of these had grown up with the sounds of country music and still preferred music that relied more on lyrics than instrumentation but they considered pure country as a thing meant for their parents. The newer sound beginning to emerge was somewhere between.

Stars started to water down the country tones and add a bit of rock elements and songs began appearing on both pop and country charts. An artist could put out an album that sounded more country this time and the next one would sound more like pop music. Every so often, one or two songs would appeal to both audiences and be picked up on radio stations playing both country and pop. Audiences began to grow as fans of one genre or the other got curious and listened to other artists they had never heard before. Those in the music industry tried to create more of the songs that became crossovers and a new branch was added to the country music tree.

As music makers on both sides began to perfect this new style, a new generation of musicians emerged. The music became known as Country Pop because it belonged in both categories. Whereas Country Rock musicians were finding it difficult to get country or rock stations to play their music,

John Denver was a major crossover star of the 1970s, whose songs like "Rocky Mountain High" and "Take Me Home Country Roads" appealed to fans of both pop and country music.

the fans embraced these new stars. Yet, nobody was ever sure exactly what to call them. One fan may say they were country while another one argued the music was definitely pop. The artists themselves tried not to choose any particular affiliation, hoping to keep fans on both sides of the argument.

The lyrics were more directed toward love songs and anything that felt good. Artists like John Denver spoke of open air, mountains, and the peace that could be found in nature. Female artists were also getting more notice, with singers like Olivia Newton-John, Anne Murray, Barbara Mandrell, Crystal Gayle, and Linda Ronstadt enjoying great success. Their softer voices spoke of love and peace of a pure nature. This purity was not to be found in another branch of country that became popular at the same time, Outlaw Country.

Outlaw Country

Willie Nelson and Waylon Jennings had been around Nashville for quite some time but they were quickly becoming disillusioned by the direction they saw country music going. They didn't like the polished sound that the new producers and artists were putting out, feeling that this new sound was a "sell-out" of the traditional sound. They saw performers in folk and rock music having greater control over their own careers. They didn't want Nashville executives to tell them what songs they could sing, or who they could perform with. They fought for the right to make music the way they wanted. When Nashville wouldn't change, they headed to west, where a new breed of country singer was developing.

In Texas, they embraced the sound that was a mixture of rockabilly and honky tonk. The lyrics told more of wild nights, fighting, drinking, prison, and bucking the system. They were soon thought of as the "outlaws" of country music, which had always embraced strong family values, love of God, and maybe an occasional night on the town. They did away with all the newer instrumentation and relied on the old standby instruments of the original country stars, guitars, fiddle, and steel guitar. Gone were the pianos and drums. The voices were harsh from alcohol and cigarettes and the music was hard and normally fast enough to dance to. Gone were the fancier country outfits and they were replaced with denim and leather jackets, dark hats, T-shirts or flannels, and cowboy boots. Some referred to this new sound as Texas Country but the term Outlaw Country struck a chord in those who played and listened and that is the term that stuck.

The original players in the outlaw country game were Willie Nelson, Waylon Jennings, Kris Kristofferson, and Merle Haggard. It wasn't long before they were joined by Johnny Cash, Johnny Paycheck, David Allen Coe, and Hank Williams Jr.

Willie Nelson helped to popularize the Outlaw Country movement in the 1970s.

At first Jessi Colter was the lone woman to be embraced by the Texas crowd, although Emmylou Harris would sometimes pop up with a duet. Then a teenager from Texas emerged on the scene. At first, Tanya Tucker had recorded in Nashville, but once she hit her late teens she gravitated toward the Outlaw Country sound. Her fans from the early years followed her.

Outlaw Country was popular throughout the seventies and eighties. As the century came to a close, the audiences saw a renewed interest as some of the younger country singers embraced the style, believing it was more true to the roots of country than what was currently coming out of Nashville. Four of the original "Outlaws," Willie Nelson, Waylon Jennings, Kris Kristofferson, and Johnny Cash, came together in 1986 to record an album titled *The Highwaymen* that is a good representation of this sub-genre.

The Quiet Period and Concert Country

When the movie *Urban Cowboy* was released in 1980, there was a renewed interest in country nightclubs and in line dancing. The Country Pop sound from Nashville remained very popular, and so did the Southern Rock sound from Georgia and the southern states. Southern Rock is very similar to Country Rock, but the lyrics and beat are a bit more electrified.

During the mid-to-late 1980s, there was a resurgence of artists who returned to the roots of traditional country music. New artists like Randy Travis, George Strait, Reba McEntire, and Emmylou Harris all had major hits with this new sound, called "neo-country." Some older country performers who had been major stars during the 1960s, such as George Jones and Conway Twitty, saw a resurgence in their popularity as the neo-country sound became popular.

In 1989, Garth Brooks emerged as a major force who would change country music forever. With his dark

Johnny Cash, the "Man in Black," is among the few artists who have been inducted in the Country Music, Rock and Roll, and Gospel Music halls of fame. Among his signature songs are "Folsom Prison Blues," "I Walk the Line," "Ring of Fire," and "Jackson," a 1963 duet with his wife June Carter Cash.

cowboy hat and raspy voice, Garth Brooks looked like an Outlaw Country artist who had gotten lost and wound up in Nashville instead of Texas. But like Elvis Presley in the 1950s, Garth would be the catalyst for change in the 1990s that increased the audience for country music.

Garth had a manner that appealed to women and made men feel they wanted to be like him. His voice was strong and could be heard throughout auditoriums and stadiums. He didn't simply stand on a stage and sing, he performed. Audiences felt that he was singing to each one personally. People wanted to watch Garth Brooks perform live, not simply listen to him sing on tape. He was the forerunner of what became known as Concert Country.

Audiences everywhere started to demand more of this kind of performance. Nashville artists who wanted to see their music sell started upgrading their stage performance, adding lights and other effects like many of the rock performers. They moved around the stage and interacted with the audience in a manner that had fallen by the roadside as Nashville moved away from small, intimate venues.

Country music was once again enjoying a wide audience as concert goers started looking at other artists that might sound like those they heard on stage. More artists, both old and news started doing concerts again, this time on bigger stages and not just at festivals and small venues. As the century came to a close, the country music artists set their sites on a much wider audience, the world.

TEXT-DEPENDENT QUESTIONS

1. What was Sam Phillips's vision for the music industry?
2. What did Gram Parsons call his style of music?
3. What is the sub-genre of country music called that allows artists to have a hit on country charts with one song but on pop charts with another? What is it called when the same song is on both charts at the same time?

RESEARCH PROJECT

Do some research on blues musicians of the late 1950s. Read about them touring Europe before the Beatles and the British Invasion started. Write a paper about what could be called a counter-invasion. How did those blues musicians affect the British Invasion that came later.

The popularity of country music has spread far beyond the United States, and performers from all over the world have found stardom in Nashville. One of them is Keith Urban, who was born in New Zealand and performed in Australia before making it big in the United States. To date, Urban has eighteen #1 hits on the American country music charts.

 WORDS TO UNDERSTAND

millennial—a person who reaches adulthood in the twenty-first century.

roundtable—a session in which several musicians who normally work independently get together on stage and take turns performing. It is much like an intimate gathering in a private home, where everyone just "goes with the flow."

virtues—positive traits that a person or people possess.

CHAPTER 4

Country Music Around the World

During World War II, musicians of the Grand Ole Opry put together a tour to travel overseas and give shows to the troops stationed in Europe or the Pacific. This was one of the first times that country music was heard outside of the United States. Travel between countries was much rarer, and country music entertainers did not do regular tours.

As country music enjoyed a resurgence in the United States during the 1990s, country music producers discovered that the rest of the world was ready to embrace American country music. Some major stars, such as Johnny Cash, were already well-known around the world. Performers like Dolly Parton consistently sold out concerts in Great Britain, Ireland, Germany, Norway, and Sweden.

In 1992, singer Don Williams was one of the first known country artists to visit Africa. He recorded his live concert and released it as an album titled *Into Africa*.

Help From the Internet

The Internet helped country music to become better known internationally. It makes it easier for musicians to reach fans and interact with them. Social media has provided a great advantage for many up-and-coming stars. Entertainers learn what fans are looking for, and fans feel connected in a way that would not be otherwise possible. By the time an artist travels to another country, they have already started to build a fan base.

YouTube and music streaming services also play large parts in gaining the interest of those thousands of miles away. These services are available just about everywhere in the free world. Many times people attending foreign universities gain access to computers while at school and get to experience new artists at minimal cost. They are able to access music, interviews and award shows. Music has always been the one thing that has no language barrier and it helps those outside the United States to feel they are closer to a culture they admire.

Younger Stars Embraced

The music of country stars like Don Williams, Dolly Parton, Garth Brooks, and Johnny Cash may be loved around world but it is the new generation of country performers that is capturing the attention of foreign audiences by conducting concert tours. This trend makes sense for a number of reasons.

The audience that is drawn to country music is younger. Almost one-third of all country music fans in the United Kingdom are **millennials**. These younger listeners can relate to the younger country performers. They come from a world that has gone through the same international upheavals, have recently graduated from college or are currently attending school, and share some of the same cultural references such as anime and video games. This common ground gives them a starting point.

Since 2012, Nashville songwriters have been taking a tour overseas and performing in **roundtable** sessions that introduce international audiences to their work. Over forty songwriters have participated so far, with the focus of the tours being on the art of writing country music. The success of these has prompted

Canadian singer/songwriter Shania Twain has sold over 100 million records, making her the best-selling female artist in country music history and one of the best-selling music artists of all time.

Nashville to take the next step with their "Introducing Nashville" tour in 2019.

This first tour will feature three performers who are also songwriters, all who have become known to country music fans in the past five years. Two of the performers, Devin Dawson and Brandy Clark, are from the United States, while Tenille Townes originates from Canada. These three are booked for a half dozen roundtable-type performances in Australia and New Zealand. If all goes as well as it is predicted, more performers will be booked for future tours.

Why Foreign Countries Love Country Music

What is it about country music that holds such high appeal to those in countries outside ours? The main reason can be found in country music's long history of standing for family and country. In a world that is often in turmoil, these things remain consistently important no matter where you travel. They are something that everyone can relate to. The details of what families and a country value may differ from one place to another, but they both remain the base for all that a person holds dear.

Country music has long held the virtues of hard work, honesty, self-reliance and equality. With more and more countries finding civil rights increasingly important, these virtues are becoming important worldwide. Young people from other countries see the slight maverick attitude country music

Scan here to learn more about International Country Music Day:

The steel guitar is an instrument often utilized in country music. It is played horizontally, with the guitarist pressing a steel or glass "slide" against the strings to create the notes. The lap steel guitar, which the performer on the right is playing here, originated in Hawaii during the late nineteenth century. In front of him is a pedal steel guitar, which is a similar instrument that has been mounted in a console with foot pedals that allow the musician to create more complex sounds.

Country star Reba McEntire shows off the special International Award she received at the 2000 Country Music Association Awards ceremony at the Grand Ole Opry in Nashville.

performers have always held toward the current status quo. They admire the tendency of America's youth to stand up and speak out and they want to embrace these qualities themselves. Country music culture enables them to feel closer to these values and gives them hope and courage to fight for what can be with persistence and faith.

"Music transcends race, nationality and creed," writes Stewart Maganga, a music journalist from the African country of Malawi. "Even country and western music, with its image of being the genre of choice for predominantly (although not exclusively) white, redneck American fans, has transcended national and even continental barriers. Country is played religiously on a number of radio stations in Africa."

Country Music Culture in Unexpected Places

It might not seem strange to find country music being enjoyed by a large audience in places like England, Australia and Canada, After all, these are countries we interact with on a daily basis. They have long been places that Americans have visited and their people have visited us. You might be surprised, however, at some of the other places that have started to not only embrace country music but have also formed their own country music communities. Let's take a look at some of the most unexpected ones.

Prague, in the Czech Republic has long been familiar to banjo players for a long time. Gibson banjos, one of the most popular brand of banjo found in country music has gotten many of its specialty design parts from the Czech Republic. This country has the distinction of being the first place outside the United States to have an all-country radio station on the air. They also have two very popular saloon-style clubs that cater to country music fans.

Africa has had at least one country station on the air since way back in the fifties. Elvis Otiena is a huge country music singer in Kenya and so is Esther Konkara. Both grew up listening to the country music station and it called to them when they were ready to embark on their own careers. Nigeria also has local country music performers such as Ogak jay Oke, Emma Ogos, and Poor Charley Akua.

Ireland having a country music presence shouldn't be too much of a surprise, after all, it was Irish and Scottish music that helped create the first country music in the Appalachian Mountains back in beginning. Some of the more popular Irish performers are Josh Ritter, the Clancy Brothers, the Irish Rovers and the Boomtown Rats.

India is another place you wouldn't associate with country music, although India's own Bobby Cash was the first Indian to record country music in Nashville. This country has seen the Bellamy Brothers touring Sri Lanka to sold out concerts, but it was Jim Reeves that first captured the attention of those in India and still holds a special seat of honor

Married in 2017, Morgan Evans and Kelsea Ballerini are rising stars in country music. Evans, born in Australia, saw his 2018 album **Things That We Drink To** *reach #1 in Australia and #9 in the United States. Ballerini has had four singles hit #1 on* **Billboard's** *US Country Airplay chart.*

in the hearts of country music fans in that country.

Argentina has its own cowboy culture. Considering it has a history much like that of the western states, this may not come as a surprise to many of those familiar with the area. Most of the country music coming from that part of the world is in the way of cover bands who play the music of Nashville country performers but there is a small number of original bands making their name in the area, especially since they have their annual country music festival that draws bands from all over South America.

The movie *The Broken Circle Breakdown* is responsible for most of the country music interest in Belgium. This movie has a ton of bluegrass culture and music throughout and its soundtrack is one of the highest selling albums in the country. This success has seen numerous country and bluegrass cover bands make appearances at establishments throughout the area.

Perhaps the most surprising country on this list is Iran. The country music scene in Iran is new and it has been a slow growth as performers have tried to break free of some of the government holds that hinder their growth. Three notable names have managed to become well-known in the area. These are Shahryar Masrour, the Dream Rovers, and Thunder. The music is a blending of both traditional country and folk music from Iran. Thunder was the first group to be allowed to record music in English. The band is a true mixing of cultures with both men and women members. Some of the band wear cowboy hats while others where traditional head scarves. This band has also been allowed to tour Europe and sold out all the shows they played. We can only keep an eye on this country music scene and see how it develops.

Australia's Country Music Culture

Australia has its own country music culture that has grown right along with that of the United States. Like the culture we have been talking about, the roots of their country music started much

Mike Denver, one of the best-known Irish country singers today, performs at the Rose of Tralee International Festival.

as ours did, with folk songs being the basis. It has grown along a similar path, with the branches being both similar yet different. The culture that has grown up around Australia's country music has readily incorporated that of the United States because the two are familiar to each other. Australia even has its very own Country Music Hall of Fame.

It is a toss-up whether Australia or Canada has a larger country music culture but both are fast approaching that of the United States. We have been able to enjoy Australian artists like

Keith Urban and Olivia Newton-John for many years and it is likely we will be hearing more from this country. The Tamworth Festival that takes place in Australia is a ten-day event. Over those ten days, it draws more than 700 artists and has 2800 events take place. The number of fans that attend has been incredible.

Festivals Around the World

Country music festivals have become very popular in many places throughout the world. These annual events draw thousands of people every year who come to listen to country music performers from not only the United States but from within their own countries as well. One of the oldest festivals has been taking place in Gstaad, Switzerland for more than thirty years.

Close to the same time period, the Country Gold International Festival in Kumamoto, Japan, has been an annual event since 1989. Another well-attended event is the Tamworth Country Music Festival in Australia. The San Pedro Country Music Festival in Argentina has been drawing crowds since 2003. This festival features country music artists from the United States, Brazil, Uruguay, Chili, and Peru. Smaller country music festivals of this type are springing up in other countries on a yearly basis.

The one country music festival that is largest in size outside the United States takes place in Britain, which has a large fan country fan base. This festival started in 2013 as a one-day event in London. That first event sold 17,000 tickets, showing what a huge draw country music has in Europe. Since then, the Country to Country (or C2C as it is now called) has grown considerably.

In March 2018, the C2C Festival took place in three cities simultaneously. Over a three-day period, performers took to the stage in London, England; Dublin, Ireland; and Glasgow, Scotland. Each performer appeared for a show on each of the three stages over the three-day period and the entire event drew over 80,000 people.

When asked why he thought country music was so popular in

INTERNATIONAL FESTIVALS

Country music festivals are springing up everywhere in the world as the Internet and musicians traveling around the world makes exposure an easy thing. Four of the largest annual country music festivals to take place outside of the United States are:

1. **Tamworth Country Music Festival in Australia**
2. **Country Gold International Festival in Kumamoto, Japan**
3. **San Pedro Country Music Festival in Argentina.**
4. **Country to Country (C2C) in Europe**

All of these feature artists from the host country as well as surrounding countries. Many of today's American artists travel to appear at these and many others throughout the world.

the United Kingdom, Ben Earle, who is half the duo known as the Shires said, "Country isn't about Stetson's and cowboys to us. It is simply about storytelling." The Shires are the first UK artists to win a Country Music Association award. They have opened the road for other UK country artists to follow. The most notable country artists from that region are Ward Thomas, Wildwood Kin, Robbie Cavanagh, and Catherine McGrath.

All of these feature artists from the host country as well as surrounding countries. Many of today's American artists travel to appear at these and many others throughout the world.

British country duo the Shires (Crissie Rhodes and Ben Earle) perform at the Isle of Wight Festival during 2017.

Nashville Is Listening

Nashville is definitely listening to what the world is asking for. With the Introducing Nashville tour in the works, more of today's young writers and performers will be making a name for themselves both hear and overseas. Artists who have established careers are finding that in order to stay on top they must embrace traveling and performing in other countries. Most aren't complaining about that!

Country music producers are also realizing that a younger audience is seeking to hear traditional style country music but with a more modern message. The old values that have long been held by the country music industry still run strong throughout the world. Instrumentation has started to go back to the more basic instruments with updated sounds. Yet, the music itself remains simple and the lyrics are given emphasis.

What lies ahead can only be greater exposure and a greater acceptance as country music reaches to embrace the differences of other cultures, while at the same time proving that at their heart, humans are all the same. They share the basic hopes, dreams, and values. It is this quality that will always ensure country music has a place in not only the music industry but in life in general.

TEXT-DEPENDENT QUESTIONS

1. What has become the largest country music festival outside the United States?
2. What country developed its own country music culture independent of the United States?
3. What country star has been the most embraced by overseas countries so far?

RESEARCH PROJECT

Do some research into what life is like for those living in the rural areas of places like Africa and Japan. Can you find similarities to life in rural areas of the United States? What are some of the main issues that families in all three areas find similar and how do you think that makes country music relatable to people in areas outside our country?

71

Carrie Underwood rose to fame after winning the fourth season of American Idol, in 2005. Since then she has released six successful albums and become one of country music's best-selling artists.

 ## WORDS TO UNDERSTAND

portmanteau—a new word created by combining parts of two other words, such as combining the words chilling and relaxing to create the word chillax.

neo-traditionalist—someone who reverts back to the more common way of doing something

stereotypical—a widely help idea of what something or someone is

CHAPTER 5

Country Music and Modern Culture

Country music has come a long way in the past one hundred years. What started out as a way for poor mountain folk to relax after a hard day of work has blossomed into a multi-billion dollar industry. Gone are the days of filling up a car trunk will recordings and traveling from radio station to radio station, playing one small bar at a time to make ends meet. Today, stars travel in luxury buses and regularly find themselves flying across the oceans to entertain the growing numbers of fans throughout the world. Listeners from all over the world tune in to hear the likes of both the older country stars and those new to the scene.

The genre has changed in many ways over the last century, but change is always necessary for growth. It has given birth to a variety of new sounds and paved the way for artists who may never have been able to share their talent with the world. Nearly every popular artist today will name at least one traditional country artist that influenced their career and many of those who enjoyed fame as rock artists in the seventies are returning to their country roots. In this chapter we will explore some of the changes that we now see in country music. We will also take a look at why this genre is enjoying such popularity among both the old and the young.

Kacey Musgraves performs in Atlanta. She has written songs that deal with subjects that are often ignored in country music, such as homosexuality and marijuana use.

Today's Women Country Singers

Women have been traditionally under-represented in music, especially country music. A few, such as Loretta Lynn, Dolly Parton, and Tammy Wynette found their way to fame in the early days but it has only been the past ten years that more women have been able to break into the traditionally male genre.

Today's women country singers aren't content with sticking with lyrics that make them seem to be nothing more than someone to support a man. Instead of sweet love songs, they have followed in the footsteps of Loretta Lynn, who challenged conventional expectations with such songs as "Fist City" and "The Pill," and speak of subjects that today's women can relate to. These cover such subjects as dealing with single parenthood, surviving domestic violence, and alcoholism.

Artists such as Jo Dee Messina, Miranda Lambert, and Kacey Musgrave represent the women who are now beginning to claim their rightful place beside their man or on their own, not following a step behind to pick up the pieces. These female artists no longer speak of standing by their man when he cheats or prefers drinking to coming home at night.

Kacey Musgrave's songs have addressed topics that are controversial in the conservative world of country music. For example, her song "Follow Your Arrow" is about gay and lesbian issues—a topic rarely discussed in the genre. Musgrave has spoken about the criticism she's received for her lyrics. "I think throwing the rebel card out there is really cheap," she told the *Wall Street Journal*. "The things I'm singing about are not controversial to me, I don't push buttons to push buttons. I talk about things that have made an impression on me that a lot of people everywhere are going through."

Today's women country singers found the path start to be paved by Loretta Lynn, who defied tradition enough to sing of not putting up with cheating or being confined to home raising babies while her man had a good time. The road was later paved by artists like Wynonna Judd and Tanya Tucker, who put aside frilly dresses and donned leather and denim that was better suited for the single parenthood they faced. The road ahead is one that is an open field for women of strength, courage, and more than a little attitude.

Television, Social Media, and Country Music

Television has played a part in launching several country music performers careers since 2005. With reality television being big, several talent shows have launched. Both winners and those who didn't win but performed well have found recording contracts as television got them the exposure they had been unable to gain except in their home towns. Stars like Carrie Underwood, Scott McCreery, Kelli Clarkson, and Miranda Lambert all got their start on competition reality shows. Miley Cyrus didn't compete on a talent show but she was a young Disney star for years. As she reached adulthood, the daughter of country heart throb Billy Ray Cyrus, ventured into country music and became a star in her own right. She has dabbled in other genres since she started but as she reaches maturity, she is returning to her country roots.

The television series *Nashville* helped spread interest in country music. It debuted in 2012 with an initial audience of 8.93 million viewers. This series would run for six seasons and be aired around the world. The story followed fictional country music stars both rising and falling in their careers and highlighted many different types of country music. Recordings were made of many of the songs from the show and released for streaming. A music special aired and many members of the cast toured both here and in the UK and Ireland. It was one of the biggest draws in getting more people to notice country music for the first time in the last decade.

While there have been no major recording stars yet that owe their success to social media, there have been several artists who have found their careers getting an initial boost from this arena. The ability to record while at home and not just in a studio has enabled many who would forever remain unnoticed to be seen my millions when they post videos of them singing on YouTube, Facebook, and other popular social media outlets. Several musicians, from many different music genres, most notably those working with Playing For Change, have found themselves becoming recognized. This group seeks out street artists from around the world and creates videos of one song that is played by all the different street artists at once in their own country. The videos are edited seamlessly, creating one song with a world of voices and instruments.

Scan here to learn more about the growing diversity of country music fans:

Fringe and Sub-Genres

Country music has always combined at least two types of music. Originally, Scottish and Irish folk songs joined with black spirituals and folk music to create the sound that was first heard by the country. Over time, influences of blues, jazz, R&B and swing became part of the genre. Western swing, Cowboy Country, Honkytonk, and Rockabilly are all examples of how various influences joined with the traditional sound to create new experiences. What remained throughout all this was the story-telling that defined the genre.

In time, Folk and Rock and Roll, and Bluegrass all split even further from the traditional sound. Different areas of the country gave rise to sub-genres that all sounded similar but had their own differences that appealed to slightly different audiences. This gave birth to such sub-genres as Zydeco, originating in the French Cajun area of Louisiana, the Bakersfield sound was a smoother version originating in California, and areas of the Southwest gave rise to Red Dirt Country. We can't forget the "bad boys and girls" of the country music arena that performed Outlaw Country, a sound that had a harder lyrics that spoke to those who lived life more on the edges of what was considered proper society. Today, there are even more **portmanteau** genres.

Today, you can find a combination of nearly every other genre mixed with a country influence. Cowpunk combines country music and punk rock and Tex-Mex combines the folk music of Mexico with the Western country along the Texas-Mexico border. Psychobilly is a mixture of goth, punk and country. Two of the most popular combinations is Pop Country, which is responsible for the large Millennial following and Country Rap. The Country Rap sub-genre is becoming ever more popular with songs like "Ghetto Country" by Mo Thugs Family, "Country Folks" by Bubba Sparxxx, and "Over and Over," which features the voices of rap star Nelly and country singer Tim McGraw. With so many variations available, there is bound to be something for everyone to enjoy in country music today.

Brian Kelley and Tyler Hubbard of Florida Georgia Line perform a concert in New York. Their music blends elements of rock and hip-hop with traditional country sounds and themes.

A Return to the Basics

Neo-traditionalists are becoming more prevalent in the world of country today. There is a sector of country music performers who are going back to the older sounds of story-telling with a more acoustic music in the background. These neo-traditionalists consist of many of those who entered the scene before the nineties.

Many of the big name performing bands of the rock genre in the seventies have returned to their country roots or are entering it for the first time in their careers. These performers believe that the rock music genre has become so divided since the nineties that it has lost its essence. They feel there is little regard for lyrics and the music is made increasingly by electronic means. Country music is offering both them and their fans a chance to feel that music still has integrity, lyrics have meaning, and talent is something that exists.

Coming Together

Country music has always been a reflection of what is going on in the world around us. From the days when coal-mining and farming dictated lyrics of a hard day's work for little pay to the open plains of a cowboy herding cattle, songs spoke of what most people could relate to. In the sixties, Vietnam and war protest songs were prevalent. When the seventies rolled around, the women's liberation movement, free love, and an expanding drug culture gave rise to music that was harsher in tone. Folk music, which spoke to the people who followed these movements became more widespread.

Today, as we see a world that is becoming more interested in finding a way to live peacefully together, those in the music industry are once again showing the world the way. The combining of many diverse genres is one way this is happening.

Singer/songwriter Chris Stapleton took home five trophies at the 2016 Academy of Country Music Awards ceremony, including Best Album (for his debut album Traveller) and Best Song (for "Nobody to Blame"), as well as awards for Songwriter of the Year, New Male Vocalist of the Year, and Vocalist of the Year.

In 2004, St. Louis rapper Nelly asked Tim McGraw to collaborate on the song "Over and Over." At the time, McGraw was one of the top stars of country music. "Over and Over" was a huge hit, reaching #1 in the United States and the United Kingdom.

Another way is in the number of duets being performed that see individuals from two very different genres blending their voices and creating a harmony that reaches twice as far as either could alone. They are showing the world as a whole that despite any differences, we are all in search of the same things in life, mainly peace, love, family, understanding, and hope.

Today's Country Fans

Who actually listens to country music? Today, it is likely that you know many people who do listen to it regularly. This may not be something some younger people readily admit because there is often stigma attached to the music. That stigma is becoming less every day, however. Today, there is actually no defining traits shared by all country music listeners.

A study in the United Kingdom showed that over one-third of country music listeners are Millennials. At any concert in the world you will find an audience made up of old and young, rich and poor, and of every culture. Country music speaks a language that almost everyone can relate to. Garth Brooks brought attention to how powerful the music can be and Dolly Parton helped take the music overseas.

The Internet is another thing that has helped spread country music. With the ability to stream music, fans are being given more of a chance to discover and download what they want and don't have to rely upon record companies and radio stations to provide the music they deem acceptable. Fans are speaking loudly on the fact they love country music and want more of it. As we saw in the last chapter, country music has spread to places as far away as the UK, Africa, Australia, and Japan and shows no sign of stopping.

 COUNTRY FAN FACTS

Country music is enjoying a wider audience than ever before and it isn't just the **stereotypical** audience of white, country-dwelling people. There are close to 4,000 radio stations that currently play only country music. A study of listeners shows that 75 percent of them owned their own home and it was valued at an average of $228,586. These listeners also had an average income above $100,000 a year. Country music fans also love concerts. In 2017, the most popular concert tour was conducted by Garth Brooks and Trisha Yearwood.

In 2018, Jason Aldean received the Entertainer of the Year award from the Academy of Country Music.

The Future

Nobody can say exactly where country music will go from here. If current trends continue, we will continue to see even more artists from different genres including country music in their acts. This will also continue to work the other way as country music fans get to experience genres they have never heard.

As the music continues gaining listeners from around the world, more country music artists from these places will find their way to our country. Women have made a firm stand and found their voice in the genre as well. It is unlikely they will settle for a background spot in the future. The "face" of country music will no longer be an old white man in jeans and a cowboy hat. It will instead be as varied as the street outside your home. A true picture of the world we live in.

TEXT-DEPENDENT QUESTIONS

1. Name three of the early women in country music.
2. Why are many of the old rock band members finding a new home in country music?
3. How many radio stations are currently playing country music?

RESEARCH PROJECT

More and more country stars are teaming up with rock performers, rap artists and other genres of musicians. Since country music has always been a reflection of what is going on in the world as a whole, write an essay that explains what this joining of musical styles says about what is happening in the world today.

CHAPTER NOTES

CHAPTER 1

p. 10: "Songwriting is fragile …" Garth Brooks, quoted in Annie Reuter, "Garth Brooks, Jason Isbell Worry About the Future of Songwriters in New Film," *Taste of Country* (April 27, 2017). http://tasteofcountry.com/garth-brooks-the-last-songwriter-trailer/

CHAPTER 3

p. 45: "Hank [Williams] had just passed …" Jason Petty, quoted in Keith O'Connor, "Country Royalty Tribute to Hank Williams and Patsy Cline Headed to Springfield," *The Republican* (March 26, 2012). https://www.masslive.com/entertainment/index.ssf/2012/03/country_royalty_tribute_to_han.html

CHAPTER 4

p. 63: "Music transcends race, nationality and creed …" Stewart Maganga, "Country Music Is Hugely Popular in Africa. But it's Nearly All Imported," The Conversation (October 15, 2017). https://theconversation.com/country-music-is-hugely-popular-in-africa-but-its-nearly-all-imported-84448

p. 68: "Country isn't about Stetsons …" Ben Earle, quoted in Karen Kay, "From Nashville with Love: How Britain Is Taking Country Music to its Heart," *The Guardian* (March 11, 2018). https://www.theguardian.com/music/2018/mar/11/country-music-uk-fans-c2c

CHAPTER 5

p. 75: "I think throwing the rebel card …" Kacey Musgrave, quoted in Megan Buerger, "Kacey Musgraves Follows Her Arrow to the Top," *Wall Street Journal* (February 13, 2014). https://blogs.wsj.com/speakeasy/2014/02/13/kacey-musgraves-im-not-everyones-cup-of-tea/

A&R department—the talent department at a record label, which is responsible for finding artists and acquiring songs for them to record. A&R stands for "artists and repertoire."

audio mixing—the process by which multiple sounds are combined into a finished song. The music producer often uses a mixing console to manipulate or enhance each source sound's volume and dynamics.

ballad—a folk song that narrates a story in short stanzas.

beat—the steady pulse that listeners feel in a musical piece.

bootleg—an unauthorized recording of a song.

chord—three or more tones played at the same time.

copyright—the exclusive legal right to control the publication or reproduction of artistic works, such as songs, books, or movies. Musicians protect their original songs through copyright to prevent other people from stealing their songs, lyrics, or musical tunes. The period of copyright protection is generally seventy years after the death of the creator of the work.

demo—short for "demonstration recording," a song that that is professionally produced and recorded to demonstrate the ability of a musician or musical group.

harmony—the simultaneous combination of tones or pitches, especially when blended into chords that are pleasing to the ear.

hook—the "catchy" part of a song that makes people want to hear it repeatedly. The hook can be lyrical or musical. It is often the title of the song, and is usually repeated frequently throughout the song.

hymn—a song of religious worship.

instrumentation—the way a song's composer or arranger assigns elements of the music to specific instruments. When done for an orchestra, this is called "orchestration."

lyrics—the words of a song.

mastering—the final process of preparing a mixed recording for commercial distribution.

measure—a way of organizing music according to its rhythmic structure. Each measure, or "bar," includes a certain number of beats.

pitch—term used to describe how high or low a note sounds. Pitch is determined by the note's frequency, or the number of complete oscillations per second of energy as sound in the form of sound-waves.

producer—the person in charge of making a record. Chooses the musicians, instrumentation, and songs for the project, and oversees it to completion, often in collaboration with the recording artist and staff of the record company.

riff—a short repeated phrase in popular music and jazz, typically used as an introduction or refrain in a song.

rhythm—a strong, regular, repeated pattern of musical sounds.

scale—a sequence of notes in either descending or ascending order.

signature song—a song that a popular music artist or band is most known for or associated with, usually one of their biggest hits. The most popular artists can have more than one signature song.

solo—a piece of music, or a passage in a piece of music, that is performed by one musician.

tempo—the speed at which a piece of music is played.

CHRONOLOGY

1922: Eck Robertson records the first commercial country records.

1923: Fiddlin' John Carson records "Little Old Log Cabin Down the Lane" and brings country music to a wider audience.

1927: The Grand Ole Opry theater opens in Nashville. The Carter Family begins recording country music.

1930: Western movies graced the movie theaters and Cowboy Country became popular with stars like Roy Rogers.

1934: Bob Wills and the Texas Playboys create their own blend of country and jazz music, which becomes known as "Western Swing."

1942: The Grand Ole Opry begins sponsoring overseas tours by country musicians to entertain American troops during the Second World War.

1948: *Billboard* magazine begins tracking the popularity of country music.

1949: Hank Williams recorded his first song with "Lovesick Blues."

1950: Patti Page records "Tennessee Waltz," the first country song to cross over to the pop charts. It ends up selling three million copies.

1953: The first BMI Country Music Awards was held.

1954: Elvis debuted. His style took much of its influence from black artists and was considered the beginning of Rock-N-Roll.

1958: Jerry Lee Lewis records "Great Balls of Fire." This crossover onto the pop charts was a huge influence that, along with Elvis and Johnny Cash, saw the growing popularity of rockabilly.

1961: The Country Music Hall of Fame inducts its first three members: Jimmie Rodgers, Fred Rose, and Hank Williams.

1960s: The Bakersfield Sound comes out of California, represented by performers like Buck Owens and Merle Haggard.

1970s: Outlaw Country explodes on the scene. Stars like Willie Nelson, Waylon Jennings, Kris Kristofferson, and Jessi Colter capture audiences with songs that talk of drinking, drugs, and wild living.

1980: The movie *Urban Cowboy* popularizes line dancing.

1989: Garth Brooks enters the scene and popularizes stadium country.

1992: Alt Country, a mixture of punk and country, becomes popular with performers such as Uncle Tupelo.

2000: The movie *O Brother Where Art Thou* renews interest in bluegrass and traditional music. African-American country star Charlie Pride is inducted into the Country Music Hall of Fame.

2010: Carrie Underwood becomes the first woman in the history of the Academy of Country Music (ACM) to win Entertainer of the Year twice.

2012: Garth Brooks is elected to the Country Music Hall of Fame.

2013: Legendary singer/songwriter George Jones dies on April 26.

2014: George Strait retires from performing after more than thirty years. Garth Brooks launches a world tour with Trisha Yearwood that last for three years.

2016: Recording of "Forever Country," a song performed by thirty of country music's most famous artists.

2017: Luke Bryan achieves a record with the most number one hits from the same album

2018: Jimmie Allen becomes the first African-American country singer to see his debut single ("Best Shot") reached the #1 spot on *Billboard's* Country Airplay chart.

FURTHER READING

Country Music Hall of Fame and Museum. *The Encyclopedia of Country Music*. New York: Oxford University Press, 2012.

Dawidoff, Nicholas. *In the Country of Country: A Journey to the Roots of American Music*. New York: Vintage, 1998.

Haggard, Merle. *Sing Me Back Home*. New York: Times Books, 1981.

Kosser, Michael. *How Nashville Became Music City USA: 50 Years of Music Row*. New York: Hal Leonard, 2006.

McDonough, Jimmy. *Tammy Wynette: Tragic Country Queen*. New York: Penguin Books, 2010.

Malone, Bill C., and Tracey E.W. Laird. *Country Music USA*, 50th anniversary ed. Austin: University of Texas Press, 2018.

Wright, Chely. *Like Me: Confessions of a Heartland Country Singer*. New York: Pantheon, 2010.

INTERNET RESOURCES

https://countrymusichalloffame.org
Website of the Country Music Hall of Fame provides information on the best of country music. It features biographies, videos, news, and more.

https://www.thefamouspeople.com/country-singers.php
Biographies of important figures in country music, both old and new, are available at this website.

https://www.youtube.com/watch?v=mzEwb9Ilq5w
This video "Lost Highway: Beyond Nashville" goes into greater detail of how far country music has traveled from its roots.

https://www.youtube.com/watch?v=9xcr1dVTcLk
Psychobilly discusses the merging of country and punk music

https://www.npr.org/sections/therecord/2018/03/20/594037569/how-the-sound-of-country-music-changed
An excellent article on how country music has changed, especially since the year 2000.

https://www.nps.gov/cham/learn/historyculture/country-music.htm
Briefly covers the history and growth of country music, including a section on regional differences in the genre.

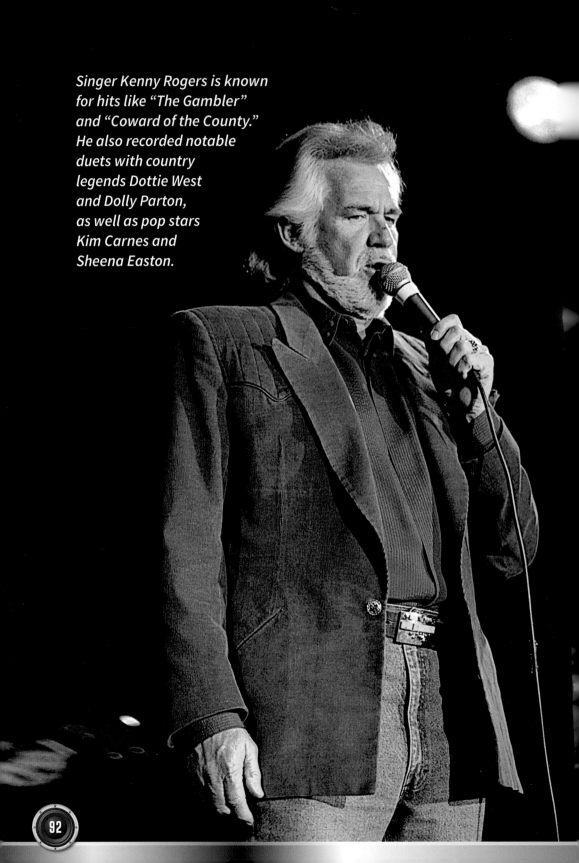

Singer Kenny Rogers is known for hits like "The Gambler" and "Coward of the County." He also recorded notable duets with country legends Dottie West and Dolly Parton, as well as pop stars Kim Carnes and Sheena Easton.

INDEX

INDEX

AUTHOR'S BIOGRAPHY

JOYCE A. ANTHONY holds a degree in Forensic Psychology but her love of country music came naturally as she stood beside her grandmother and sang the old mountain songs to the sound of a harmonica. Her roots in the mountains of Pennsylvania have never dimmed even though life has taken her to the city. She has written several books, homeschooled and rescued a mini-zoo, in addition to getting her degree.

CREDITS

Courtesy Birthplace of Country Music Museum: 28; Everett Historical: 13, 32, 38; Library of Congress: 22, 42, 53; courtesy Old Time Blues: 31; used under license from Shutterstock, Inc.: 11; Steve Broer / Shutterstock.com: 50; Creative Jen Designs / Shutterstock.com: 15; DFP Photographic / Shutterstock.com: 69; Featureflash Photo Agency / Shutterstock.com: 8, 18, 62; D. Free / Shutterstock.com: 81; Kathy Hutchins / Shutterstock.com: 36, 64, 80; Paul Keeling / Shutterstock.com: 66; Aija Lehtonen / Shutterstock.com: 61; MPH Photos / Shutterstock.com: 72; Neftali / Shutterstock.com: 44; Lev Radin / Shutterstock.com: 59; Mark Reinstein / Shutterstock.com: 92; Rena Schild / Shutterstock.com: 46; Joe Seer / Shutterstock.com: 40; Bart Sherkow / Shutterstock.com: 48; Jamie Lamor Thompson / Shutterstock.com: 74; Josh Withers / Shutterstock.com: 52; Debby Wong / Shutterstock.com: 6, 56, 79, 83; Southern Folklife Collection: 26; courtesy Stricklin Family: 33; Wikimedia Commons: 24; Aleksandr Atkishkin / Dreamstime.com: 7, 23, 37, 57, 73; BiancoBlue / Dreamstime.com: 20; Pop Nukoonrat / Dreamstime.com: 34; Jrtmedia / Dreamstime.com: 54; Kyolshin / Dreamstime.com: 70.